Polished Passionate & Poised

Memoirs for The World Changer

Published By: Life With A View Publishing Company

Designed By: GermanCreative

Biblical Reference Unless otherwise noted, scripture reference were taken from the King James Version of the Holy Bible. Scriptures taken from Holy Bible.

Brainyquote retrieved September 17, 2019 at
https://www.brainyquote.com/topics/passion-quotes

Gateway Bible retrieved September 17, 2019 at
https://www.biblegateway.com/

Table of Contents

iii

Dedication

This book is dedicated to anyone that has had the drive to be a world changer. You the reader of this book have already taken the necessary steps to becoming a world changer just by having this book in your hands. Initially for those who have started out strong as a world changer but for some reason or another you have become distracted. This book will ignite your passion again. So, for this my prayer is that God gives you increase as you go along your journey as a world changer. May your passion run like wildfire just as this scripture Isaiah 6:8 (NLT) says, "Then I heard the Lord asking, 'Whom should I send as a messenger to this people? Who will go for us?' I said, "Here I am. Send me." God is looking for volunteers. How About You? Are you looking to be that volunteer world changer?

Secondly, I want to dedicate this to my husband, children and grandchildren and future generation that are to come that will shine bright as that valued diamond.

Acknowledgements

I want to thank God who is the author and finisher of my life. I shall continuously give him honor and praise for all his gifts that he has placed within me. This journey has been through some tough times, BUT GOD allowed everything to happen to mold, and reshape me to the desired woman I am today. This is how the birthing of Polished, Passionate & Poised has become a reality.

I want to express my sincere gratitude for all the contributors to this project from Dr. Tasheka Green for the fire burning foreword you have written for this book. My Co-Authors Lia Abney, Royshonda Boulden, Linette Howard, Cherry Moaney, Sharon Cooper Mizell, Robin. M. Sample, Sherone Thompson and Ira Warren. Thank you for entrusting me to carrying on this vision and coming forth with a yes…. I pray and speak double blessings to each of you my beautiful sisters.

I humbly extend to all that have believed and supported the IAM2INSPIRE vision.

Foreword

*P*olished, *Passionate, and Poised* is a collaboration of testimonies and stories that provide evidence to the verse of scripture in Job 23:10 (NIV), "But he knows the way that I take; when he has tested me, I will come forth as gold." As the title of this book states, we are *"Polished"*, improved and refined, *"Passionate"*, full of fervent ambition, and *"Poised"*, self-assured with confidence and grace.

Being *Polished, Passionate, and Poised* is what comes after a series of events take place to merely bring out the best in you. With that being said, being *Polished, Passionate, and Poised* does not come without a cost. No value can be placed on the processes in which life brings to mold you in becoming what you were created to be. But in the end, you will realize that you are so precious in the eyes of God, that He thought kindly of you to permit this test, knowing that you have the power, love, and fullness to endure, go through, and come out as pure gold.

Even this very moment, you may be going through something in your life, and the pressure and heat have intensified. There may be more questions than answers, and more days of isolation, than days of celebration; but be still and know, that this is just a part of the process, that is designed to refine you into the precious masterpiece you were created to become. There is no test, challenge, force, or obstacle that you cannot overcome. You have everything on the inside of you to grab hold of faith and latch onto hope to obtain the promises for your life. The pressure, intensity, and heat will extract the things in your life that hinders you from reaching your destiny and remove any elements that distort your vision. During this process, it does not feel good, looks good, and even sounds good, but it is necessary because the tests, challenges, forces, or obstacles come before the promotion and the elevation.

The tests, challenges, forces, or obstacles are making you more *Polished, Passionate, and Poised*, and provides you the evidence of your composition. For your price is far above rubies; you are precious and valuable in God's eyes. You are fearfully and wonderfully made, and marvelous is the work of God that will be birthed through you. God wants you to understand your worth and to purify all the things holding you back from obtaining the fullness of His promises for your life.

In becoming *Polished, Passionate, and Poised*, there will be many tests, challenges, and forces, in which you have to endure to get to a place of refinement, attainment, and stand in a posture of courage and hope. However, you stand firm, grounded in the belief that life processes did not come to break you, rather it was sent to make you. The tests were not designed to consume you, rather it was designed to change you. The challenges were not your opposition but rather placed you in a position of prayer. The forces were not designed to destroy, but rather to deliver you to a place of peace, joy, and liberty. And the obstacles will not block you, but it opens a door of opportunity in which no man can shut.

I am honored to write the foreword of this book, not only because Visionary Author Michelle Hammond is passionate about exemplifying the qualities of a servant leader, through her words and deeds, but she is an authentic example of a woman who is dedicated to using her voice to share testimonies of her tests, challenges, life struggles from birth defect, low self-esteem, and mental abuse to help others. Michelle and I share the same belief that purpose is not what you can gain, rather it is what you can give, and how your giving plants seeds of hope, that blossoms into an abundance of goodness for others. For the measurement of greatness is determined by how many people you help and serve. As you grow, others should grow. As you become successful, your success should bless others more than it blesses you. As you get better, situations around you begin to transform. As your mind shifts, your life will too. Greatness, growth, success, better, and shifts, cannot come if you are not *Polished, Passionate, and Poised* and or go through the process to become *Polished, Passionate, and Poised.*

Therefore, this book will help you to develop an understanding of the fact that all that you are and will ever become has nothing to do with you. Being *Polished, Passionate and Poised* is for others to see your light, and know that the glory came with a story, the effect came with a cause, the reward came with a price, and the product was the result of a process. For the process is what you need to understand who you are from the inside out, rather than the outside in.

I hope this book helps you to understand the principles of becoming *Polished, Passionate, and Poised* and walk out this journey fearlessly and full of courage. I hope that you will see yourself as God sees you; as a great leader, influential entrepreneur, inspirational speaker, profound teacher, transformational coach, a motivational macro-voice in the earth, virtuous woman, wise wife, matriarchal mother, servant, and an answer to others who need of you.

In closing, as you embark upon the journey in becoming *Polished, Passionate, and Poised,* you have to undergo a processing that will bring out the best in you. In becoming *Polished Passionate, and Poised*, you have to be able to withstand the fire and know that you will not be burnt. In becoming *Polished, Passionate, and Poised*, you have to be obedient to what is being required of you. And in becoming *Polished Passionate, and Poised*, you have to have the courage to go all by yourself and know that you are in the plan of God. For your faith and trust will sustain you through the process. God will give you strength for the wait, and grace for the journey.

For God is the writer of these stories, Michelle Hammond, along with the contributing authors in this book share the chapters of their life, in which they have undergone the process of becoming *Polished, Passionate, and Poised*. These stories will inspire you to find courage in knowing that if you maintain your integrity and stay committed to your destiny, you will come out *Polished, Passionate, and Poised*.

If you are still here, go and live a *Polished, Passionate, and Poised* life.

Dr. Tasheka L. Green
President, Founder & Chief Executive Officer
To Everything There is a Seasons, Inc.
www.2eseasons.com
1.866.475.3178
@2ESEASONS

PROTECTED DIAMOND

Michelle Boulden Hammond

We all at one point of time have journeyed into a jewelry store looking at all the different clusters of diamonds located in the showcases they are being held. Have you ever taken in consideration of just how smooth the retail salesperson is just to get that sale? He or she may ask that question "Would you Like to Try It On"? Well this is the starting point of embarking on the decision-making process should I buy and how much will it cost. When holding this precious jewel called the diamond have you ever considered the process this precious stone goes through to get its valued beauty and rarity. What you see at the jewelry store is the finished process of the diamond durability, but this rare gem has endured hardness, toughness and stability. I too have been through a similar process just like a diamond, but it was for my making to follow through with the God given gift of compassion and willingness to serve. However, a diamond is relatively brittle and will chip or fracture if is not handled and protected against shock. So, in the following story you will read about my journey of how through some rough and hard times I learned to "Protect My Diamond".

In my beginning stages of life as a small child my polishing period was then a tectonic factor that would help me become the poised leader I am today. Some today may find it difficult to believe that I had been born with a deformity with both my legs and feet. I still have the corrective shoes today that are almost fifty years old located on my nightstand. There is not a day that doesn't go by that I look at these shoes as a reminder to say, "Thank God I don't look like what I've been through." According to the scripture Psalm 37:23 *The steps of a good man are ordered by the Lord, and He delights in his way.* In this period of my life I would say that this would be like the diamond being uprooted and transformed. I believe that the adversary thought his plan would work, to have me crippled to destroy the assignment and the plan for my life. God stepped in and blocked that alternative plan with protecting his diamond. He gave me a new walk for the assignment ahead. I had mentioned briefly that in my youth I was challenged with a birth deformity, but I left out a small bit of information. The information I didn't disclose earlier was that I was adopted at the tender age of eighteen months old. I mention this part of my story because so many people do not understand all the emotional stress a child feels when learning they are adopted. I can say that today I am a "Recovered Adoptee". You see I was raised by two wonderful parents that were relatives to my biological mother. My parents disclosed to me at the age of ten that they had adopted me. It was a great shock to me on this day to learn this news. It felt at that present moment that I was from another world and everything around me became blurred. Many questions such as Who Am I? Why did my biological mother give me away? Therefore, I will tell you sometimes in my life I often thought about what life would have been like if I had not been adopted. From what I had discovered it was for my best interest that I was displaced from the current living situation with my biological mother into a good and safe home. Again, I see that God once again protected the diamond.

When we think about great leaders do you think they are just born? That is a question answered with the cliché of leaders are not born; they are made shaped from their experiences. So, in my experiences of childhood trauma, mental abuse, rejection they have been aligned to move me to the diamond I am today.

Polishing Factor

It was when I realized that everything, I went through prior was not for me, but to testify and help someone else who has had the same issues. I must honestly tell you this did not happen overnight. It was a process that many times I found myself repeating the same cycle until I learned to let go and let God. A prime good example of this would be a few months before the construction of this book I meant a young lady at More Than Java coffee house located in Laurel, MD. I was on my way to do a radio show interview and stopped there for lunch. This young lady came and introduced herself to me and shared that she was there on behalf of her book signing. I shared with her that I was an author as well. She disclosed that her book was about her emotional transitions she went through as an adoptee. I was in total amazement this was the perfect opportunity for me to share my thoughts. At that moment I felt a release and started calling out to her saying; I bet you felt as though you had a double life? Did you have problems with rejection. She responded yes to all the questions. This clearly was a divine connection for me healing permanently. See I had thought that all these years I had really dealt with my true feelings on my adoption process, but truthfully, I only had buffed that area of my life. Which meant that I only removed a thin layer of the surface. However, God intervened with me meeting this young lady to help me heal by becoming polished. You as the reader take a moment to think of the key experiences that have shaped you as a leader. It is my prayer that stories are already coming into your mind.

So, in the qualities of being polished we must make necessary steps to be aware that it's not about what you do, it's about how you do it. In everything we do we must have integrity and be authentically honest with ourselves first. Initially when being authentic we generally are speaking about being true, real and original not fake. In this society today we do not need any more counterfeit leaders. When we are being this authentic polished diamond, we are being this rare and valuable jewel. If you can remember earlier, I had mentioned the smooth tactics the jeweler uses to get that purchase of the diamond. As the purchaser you clearly want a diamond not cubic zirconia. There are many purchasers waiting for your hidden treasure to help them to their destinations. So, when we are displaying our leadership character in the polished diamond capacity, we must give the real not pretending to be someone we aren't. So, protect your diamond so you can be displayed in the showcase.

Essential Steps for Your Polished, Passionate and Poised Journey:

❖ Know yourself - Accept the flaws and all and be comfortable with yourself. Yes, we sometimes would like to tune out the things we don't want to hear. If we don't truly understand ourselves and know who we are it is time to dig deeper and find the resolution. So, I will give you a reference to what the word of God says that you are: "I am God's workmanship, created in Christ to do good works that He has prepared for me to do (Ephesians 2:10

❖ Recognize where you don't have strong boundaries – As a leader we must know the signs to recognize when we don't have boundaries. This is important because when boundaries aren't set this can lead to letting others tell you how to act, feel and think. Remember God has placed a treasure within you and not setting boundaries could lead to you missing out on your assignment. Initially health wise in long term this could lead to frustration and depression because you will feel unfilled or lost.

❖ Do things you love – The overall mechanism of the statement is LOVE. This speaks volume that resonates joy, peace and happiness. When we find ourselves doing what we love it helps us to brand new avenues of motivation. The general key will be that you will prosper by seeing the world for all it is, and you'll be more successful and become that polished person God attended you to be. A question to keep in your memory database "*Will someone who cross my path change because they see me doing what I love?*"

❖ Help someone else-I truthfully will tell you this is one of the standards that I continuously to use daily. Do you know that there are research studies conducted that typically states that when we find ourselves helping others that we can extend our lifespans?

Secondly when someone extends offering to help someone it can offset a chain reaction of other acts of kindness. This ripple effect can be the start throughout the community, and then worldwide.

My prayer for you the reader

Heavenly father I first acknowledge and thank you for allowing your gift of creativeness for this book Polished Passionate and Poised come to a reality. I ask that you bless the holder of this book. It is my prayer that this will enhance them to be that polished rare diamond that shines brightly. Let the leader within be released in an authentic poised way to be a world changer for the kingdom. We thank you and bless your name.

Amen

DIAMOND IN THE ROUGH

Royshonda Boulden

"one having exceptional qualities or potential but lacking refinement or polish"

When I was a little girl, I could remember being asked often "What do you want to be when you grow up?", with my spunky personality and innocence I'd smile and answer happily "A ballerina!" and then proceed to show off my not so trained moves. As a kid, I felt no worries, no stress or thoughts about the future. Everything was pure innocence. I grew up being raised by a village, which I am forever grateful for. My mom and Dad had a great support team which helped mold me into the woman I am today. Trust me, life hasn't always been easy, nor did I ever become a ballerina, but I'm a living testimony to prove that God is indeed just who he says he is. I've broken generational curses and defeated many battles that were thrown out to destroy me. But deep down inside I knew, I had a purpose and a story to tell. First, I learned to break this burden of being "perfect", because I felt like I had to prove something to every person I came across. Until one day, I decided that I would no longer let others dictate who I am and my journey in this thing called life. I've always been labeled with so many names like "quiet", "sneaky" and "shy". Or on a positive note "princess", "good girl" and "pretty". How could an individual such as myself handle positive and negative comments and balance it out daily? Well, I did and even though I continued to smile and remained a happy individual, many never knew the demons I fought all alone. Those demons kept me quiet physically, mentally and emotionally and I struggled to figure out who I was and my purpose in life. If I couldn't help myself, I figured I could always help the next person in need and someway, somehow, that would ease any pain I'd ever endure.

My childhood wasn't a bad one. I was loved by many, and in most cases was your typical spoiled little girl. As a child, you look for love, trust and safety, so by any means you are more vulnerable when it comes to affection. Although I was raised by a village, it didn't mean everyone in that village had good intentions. From ages of five to eleven years old, I experienced being molested by two males during that period. Today, I would've told my younger self to speak up, but for years I held that secret to myself. I never knew that what I experienced would change the way I processed things or express myself emotionally. No one knew what happened to me, not even my parents. I kept this secret for years until I learned to trust again fully and acknowledged that I was victim, not the offenders. After being molested, I struggled with self-esteem issues. As a female in general we learn that our bodies go through changes. I can remember being in high school and skipping out on lunch and only eating when I got home from school. My self-esteem was at a very low point after growing up remembering being called "chunky", "chubby" and "fat" and although to others, it may have been a joke, it meant that I wasn't appealing to the eye. I struggled with eating once a day to barely eating at all, unless I was told to. The thought of pursing anorexia had flashed across my mind on numerous occasions. I wanted to be thin, like the models and video girls I would see on television growing up. I wanted to be accepted. So if starving myself was going to help me become successful, then I'd do it. I knew I was at the age where sex was huge for my age group. But thankfully, my morals and good mentors allowed me to see the beauty in myself inside and out. If it wasn't for my mother, I also wouldn't know the value of my beauty. She instilled in her children as much as she could how special, beautiful or awesome we were. Life wasn't easy, it isn't easy. But one thing I've learned is to be open to take everything as a lesson learned. Dealing with past issues can put a burden on how you progress in life. After everything I've endured that was meant to hurt me in the process, I learned that I suffered from anxiety. I couldn't explain why my mind would race, why I was so irritable, cranky, and at times felt like I wanted to scream. When we don't deal with certain issues, it begins to eat at us. During my journey through adulthood, I really had to do some soul searching. Also, acceptance. I couldn't change the environment I was exposed to, or the things I went through, but I was able to change what I would allow in my life and what I wouldn't allow. I am here today because I learned that my journey was just that important. I learned through therapy to just let go and embrace life itself. Learning to live for yourself and what your purpose is, is one of the best feelings ever. One thing I learned about life, we have gifts. If we don't use them, we lose them. I knew I had a love for writing when I was in high school. I began writing poems, which helped me to express myself when I had a hard time doing so vocally. From poems, I found an interest in writing stories which allowed me to use my imagination, just as I did when I was a kid. Writing helped me to escape the negativity that may had been clustering my young mind and became a positive outlet. In high school, I had an opportunity to write a play for the drama club, which I turned down twice due to fear. I know many say never have any regrets, but that is one thing I absolutely regret not doing. Writing also gave me the opportunity to write a poem for my college black history month program which was added in the local newspaper that year. It also gave me a voice, to speak for those who have been afraid to speak up. Of course, I'm just now taking the steps to get back into writing, but I am super passionate about doing so. I consider myself a diamond in the rough as I went through my tests and trials. I didn't know my worth and my purpose when all along I was a diamond awaiting to be polished. You see, although I went through many trials, God had his hands on me the entire process. I had to learn that without faith, I have nothing. There were many areas of my life where I've doubted the works of what he could do. When I speak about generational curses, I speak on the negative tongues that spoke teenage pregnancy and promiscuous activity on my name. Despite issues of alcoholism in my family, I survived. Despite being called "not smart enough" I manage to graduate high school and became a college graduate while pursing another degree. I defeated what was meant to break me. In life, we learn to grow. I know I've had times where I have aimed to be perfect, but I'm just enough because I believed in myself and what I could do. To anyone who feels like there is no way out, keep fighting, keep pushing because there is a way.

LET THE POLISHING BEGIN

Cherry Moaney

You can't hold me down, you can't hold me down, you can't hold me down! That is my motto! I have been through the fire and I came out without smelling like smoke or looking burnt. I have bent to the point of almost breaking, but I didn't break. That is nothing but the grace of God that I don't look like what I have been through. You see I was molested as a child and date raped as an adult. I should have lost my mind when I was being molested. I could have lost my life while I was being date raped. Oh, the pressure of having to carry all that around as a child, then as an adult. God has been polishing me for a while, which has made me passionate about serving Him and helping others become poised individuals.

Under Pressure

Let me introduce myself. My name is Cherry and I am a survivor, overcomer, warrior, and a diamond in transition. Why a diamond you say? Diamonds go through so much pressure to become one of the most beautiful and sought-after gems in the world. The whole process can be what we would call violent if we witnessed the entire thing. That was me, years ago. Going through the pain of being molested with anything he could find to put his hands on and not screaming. Pressure! Having to be in the same room as he was during family get togethers. Pressure! Wanting to cry and knowing that I couldn't. Pressure!

Date rape was another violence that I had to endure. Pressure! Imagine going out on a date for the first time with a man that seemed genuine and he forces himself on you. Pressure! He picked me up and we went to dinner and a movie and when I thought I was on my way home; he took another turn to a wooded area. The pressure is building! He said he would make my life a living hell if I breathed a word to anyone. Oh, the violent pressure of that night! The pressure was so bad I could have lost my life. I asked myself how I was ever going to make it past the violence that I had endured.

The pressure, the pressure, the pressure. The pressure was so hot that I thought I was going to burst. This young girl, having been through so much violence, was still standing. No one knew what this young girl had been through because I didn't let anyone see it. I only let people see the outside they were not allowed to really see me on the inside. I held it together for many years. No one knew the violence I had endured, except the person that experienced it with me and that was my sister. How was this young girl going to make it? I never understood why this happened to me. Why was I the one that all these horrible things happened to? I thought God said He loved me. I thought God loved children. These are the thoughts that I was having as I was growing up.

Where Is The Passion?

I felt guilty for a long time about what happened to me. I felt like everything that happened to me was my fault. I started thinking about what I may have done wrong and how I had caused these people to do these horrible things to me. I thought maybe I shouldn't have worn that outfit or maybe I shouldn't have acted like that. I was trying to come up with excuses as to why it was my fault. Then I started thinking, wait a minute I was a kid. I wasn't doing anything but being a kid. Constantly going through the guilt that plagued me caused me to shut down.

I shied away from people, to the point that I went into a state of seclusion. I tried to make myself unnoticeable. I always stayed in the back of everything. I was never in the forefront because I always felt people could see the filthiness on me. I felt they could smell all the bad things that happened to me. I didn't want people to see me or get close enough to me to smell me. I wanted people to think I had it all together.

As a child I always felt like I didn't belong. I was with my family, but I felt they weren't my family. Not because they had done anything to me, but that was where my brain was at the time. I never felt like I fit in with anyone. I started rejecting my family. I stopped going to family functions, feeling like they were rejecting me. My mind was telling me they were rejecting me when they had nothing to do with my state of mind. Just because I wasn't included in some of the conversations, I felt they were rejecting me. I moved further and further into my own world. I was content in my world because I could control it. I didn't have to let anyone in that I didn't want in.

The pain started to take root. I would sit and cry sometimes and not even know why I was crying. I was in so much pain and I didn't even know it. I had found a way to mask the pain that I was feeling. I pushed it to the back of my mind and became the person that I thought people expected me to be. I lost me in the pain.Things got so bad for me that I had to see a therapist. I didn't want to at first, because I didn't want people to think there was anything wrong with me. I know the stigma of my culture. I didn't want people to think that I was crazy. I soon got past that my first visit. It felt so good to be able to talk to someone and they do not pass judgement on me. Yes, I could have talked to my sister or a friend, but they are my loved ones and they may not have given me the advice that I needed because they didn't want to hurt my feelings. I needed someone that would be honest with me even if it hurt my feelings. I kept going back week after week, after week. I learned that the things that happened to me were not my fault. I learned that in order to help myself I had to go back to where the trauma happened. I had to first go back to that little 10-year-old girl that got molested and love her past all the hurt and pain she suffered. That was the most difficult thing that I had to do, but I did it and I am glad I did. I am a better person because of that. I loved her to the young woman that got date raped. I hit a stumbling block there because I had so much guilt and shame because I was an adult and I should have known better. I worked through all this. I put a lot of work and homework into making me a better person. The goal was to get me to become the best me that I can be.

I noticed my confidence coming back. I was becoming more involved in church and learning about God. I became confident that I am a child of God. As much violence as I went through, I am confident there is a God. He was the only one that could have gotten me through the pain, shame, guilt, and rejection. Growing in God gave me the confidence in knowing that I could overcome anything. Philippians 4:13 ESV states, "I can do all things through Him, who strengthens me". The more I read the scripture, the more confident I became. The more I believed. It woke a passion in me that had been lying dormant for a long time. That passion was education. I became so confident that I went back to school. I signed up for college. I was so excited I could see my passion re-emerging. I became the student that others looked up to. I was always early and always prepared. I felt like I was back in high school. I was finding my voice again. I was rediscovering who I was. I was learning to love me again. My passion for education was returning, but a new passion had emerged. That passion was to serve God. Without Him none of this would have been possible. I will forever be grateful of the day that I decided I was going to serve God.

Poised for Greatness

The leader was starting to stand up. As I was becoming more confident, the leader in me was standing up. I was going through transitioning from one church to another. As my passion for serving God was growing so was my desire to become more intimate with Him. It was then that I met Apostle John Cornish Sr. one day in the store and he invited me to his church, St. John's Family Worship Center. I didn't go right away, I waited awhile. When I did go, I got an awakening that I didn't know was lying dormant. I started to learn who I was. I was around people that saw things like I did, heard things like I did, and felt things like I did. I was learning who I was in Christ. I was a saved woman, but I

15

needed to learn more about God and where I fit into His Kingdom plan. I needed to know what my assignment is in God's Kingdom. I was able to identify some of the gifts and talents that I possess under Apostle's leadership and I am grateful for the guidance and direction that I received under his care.

When I arrived at Kingdom Life Fellowship Ministries I was broken. Some things had happened in my life to question whether I was hearing God or hearing man. I kept attending church and over time I started to feel like I belonged there. I joined the ministry and it has been full steam ahead.

It has been under the leadership that I feel I have started to evolve into the person God has called me to be. Pastor Jerome Trott, Jr. is my leader. His wife Pastor/Evangelist Rhonda Trott is my mentor. Pastor Rhonda, as I call her, has been the motivation that I have needed to pull out of me what God has put in me. She is teaching me to be that strong woman of God that the Lord can use. The teachings that she gives to the members is phenomenal, but the Words of Wisdom that she gives the Daughters of Destiny are mind changing and life changing. Pastor Rhonda is such a strong woman and she is teaching me how to become a more effective leader. I have learned a lot about integrity and humility. Humility has been the hardest thing to learn because I know I can't do the things I used to do. I must wait for God even though I want to jump right in with my own answers.

Becoming a minister has allowed me to be surer of myself. Learning that I am not, nor was I ever defeated. I am confident that what I endured was so I could help someone today that is going through the same issue that I went through. My intent is to help someone realize that the pressure that they are enduring is well worth it.

The pressure allows us to rise to the top. We can't see it when we are going through our go through, but it is there. Each violent act that I went through was a layer of pressure. The pressure kept pushing me higher and higher to the top.

There is a level of endurance that I had to learn. If you truly want God to help you get through, you must be prepared to endure it. You got to believe that you are coming out with the victory on the other side. This is hard to do especially when you are in the middle of the storm. Thank God for Isaiah 43:1-2 ESV, "When you pass through the waters, I will be with you; and through the rivers, they shall not overwhelm you; when you walk through fire you shall not be burned, and the flame shall not consume you". I know this now, but when I was going through, I had no clue what was going on. If you keep pressing you will get to your NOW season. Pastor Rhonda, keep pushing and stretching me because God is not through with me yet.

I am still going through the polishing because I feel like there is more work that needs to be done. Through this whole process I have become more passionate about my work in the Kingdom that I need to do and pleasing God. I don't take any credit for the person that I have become. I am an atmosphere changer on my way to becoming a world changer. This hidden gem has been found and she is polished, passionate, and poised to take on the world.

MY DIAMOND LIFE

Sharon Cooper Mizell

The journey of a sheltered, little girl from a small town on the Eastern Shore of Maryland, Coppersville, was and has been the framing of the entitlement of this book "Polished, Passionate, Poised". I've pondered in my heart for many years as a child these questions until just a short time ago – "who am I, and why am I here (purpose)?" Through this journey that I've been enduring and persevering in by the grace of my Lord Jesus Christ, those questions have become my life's story "Enjoying My Journey"; and, this book shares a synopsis of the process of my and every soul's metaphor as a diamond being "polished, passionate and poised" for the brilliance of light to shine the glory of God and for others to follow.

Early in the season of caregiving for my husband, I began to take notice closer to my inner emotions and feelings as they would arise during certain situations. I chose not to dismiss them from my thoughts anymore, especially because they were areas that I had not been introduced or ventured into. During this period, my thoughts of value to my life was diminishing. I had always been a shy, introverted person, taught to treat everybody with love. I did not like confrontations even when I knew that I was being treated wrongfully. It was easier to back off and stay away from the situation and/or people. The daggers of life became more and more intense--from areas that I would have never suspected to have received from—family, friends and even church folk. My prayer life with God became more and more steadily and intimate. As I sojourned onward, the Spirit of God reminded me of His Word as to who I am: Psalm 139:13-16 and Genesis 1:26:27,

"For you formed my inward parts;
you knitted me together in my mother's womb.
I praise you, for I am fearfully and wonderfully made.
Wonderful are your works;
my soul knows it very well.
My frame was not hidden from you,
when I was being made in secret,
intricately woven in the depths of the earth.
Your eyes saw my unformed substance;
in your book were written, every one of them,
the days that were formed for me,
when as yet there was none of them."

"Then God said, "Let us make man in our image, after our likeness. And let them have dominion over the fish of the sea and over the birds of the heavens and over the livestock and over all the earth and over every creeping thing that creeps on the earth. So, God created man in his own image, in the image of God he created him; male and female he created them."

Not that this was an after-thought, but I was a new believer in Christ. I grew up in the church but didn't know the meaning nor the understanding of salvation through Christ. I later received Christ as my Lord and Savior on Palm Sunday,

1995. I continued to ponder in my heart and mind, what, why, and where these feelings (bitterness, angry, resentment, outspoken, etc.) were coming from. As I continue to grow in the grace and knowledge of God, the answer to these questions stated prior is—sin. This three-letter word is the nature of my (mankind's) natural being.

> "Behold, I was brought forth in iniquity,
> and in sin did my mother conceive me.
> Behold, you delight in truth in the inward being,
> and you teach me wisdom in the secret heart."
> **Psalm 51:5, 6**

But my spiritual birth through Christ Jesus, I've received His assurance that,

> "…God is light, and in him is no darkness at all. If we say we have fellowship with him while we walk in darkness, we lie and do not practice the truth. But if we walk in the light, as he is in the light, we have fellowship with one another, and the blood of Jesus his Son cleanses us from all sin. If we say we have no sin, we deceive ourselves, and the truth is not in us. If we confess our sins, he is faithful and just to forgive us our sins and to cleanse us from all unrighteousness. If we say we have not sinned, we make him a liar, and his word is not in us."
> **1 John 1:5-10**

As I've continued this pathway set before me, God has inspired me to study the life of a "Diamond" (approximately 10 years ago to present). Throughout this study by an appointed time, He has continued to reveal by knowledge and understanding numerous areas of my inner being that are to emerge from the depths of my soul through the process of life in this world. This is one of many beginning processes of a new believer's life eternal with Christ just as the diamond's process in producing a precious stone.

The sharing of this metaphor is taken from the writings of Sam Jacobson, Meaningful Life Center, "A Lesson from Diamonds: Every Person is a Diamond" (meaningfullife.com/every-person-is-a-diamond.com). In every process of creation and/or development, there are steps.

> "The steps of a man are established by the LORD,
> when he delights in his way;
> though he fall, he shall not be cast headlong,
> for the LORD upholds his hand."
> **Psalm 37:23, 24**

> "Trust in the Lord with all your heart,
> and do not lean on your own understanding.
> In all your ways acknowledge him,
> and he will make straight your paths."
> **Proverbs 3:5, 6**

Through my journey which I've been enjoying, despite the thorns and thistles along the way accompanied with a bed of roses, this book, "Polished, Passionate, Poised" gives light to me and all my sisters' (Author & Co-Authors) being that precious gem.

Most diamonds are found deep beneath the earth's surface and need to be excavated from molten rock just as the true essence of each of our souls. The worth of man's soul is great in the sight of God. His love for us is infinite and extends to all. Just as I was suffering from the issues of life (lack of self-confidence, intimidated by others due to not having my father present in the home and various temporal items), I too needed and continuously need to be reminded that my soul's worth is as precious as a "diamond".

After surrounding rock is crushed, what remains is the diamond in rough. Throughout this process in my life, I endured an even more intensity of manipulation, intimidation, and domination which harden my heart to not trust to the receiving of love from others while continuously displaying love to others as always taught. I always felt in my heart that I could never be truly loved by anyone. But as time has its value to man's development of life, the process of cutting and splitting along the grain of our inner being begins the forming of the precious gem (the soul). Through the pain of cutting and splitting away at the hardness of heart, mind, and soul of my life, the intimacy of love from God, being my Shepherd (Psalm 23), begins to deepen and show forth a light of love, faith, and understanding to my disappointments, brokenness, and frailties as an overcomer.

The steps of "polishing" begins to allow the facets to emerge. Through this process the facets are ground on the surface which bears a paste of diamond dust and olive oil. As each facet is cut, it requires a changing of position of the stone in the holder. My relations to this step continues to be very memorable as I've had to endure and persevere through many trials (in a tragic accident losing of a very close church family member, becoming disabled, job lost, 15+ years caregiving for my veteran husband until death along with presently caring for my disabled veteran daughter, Psychia) to name a few. Each one has repositioned me into areas of spiritual growth in my life (purification, motivation, sanctification) which has given me: a deeper appreciation for and understanding of my relationship with Christ; revealed the dark areas that wants to continue to plaque my life. But as my inner being is being polished day-by-day with Jesus's love, the purpose of my journey begins to refract, reflect and disperse light just as the final product of brilliant crystals. A diamond has four characteristics which determines its value, carat (weight), color, clarity, and cut. Most of them are polyhedrons, have many surfaces (facets). During the polishing process they are converted into many more facets, and the most popular being the "brilliant cut," having 58 facets. Throughout the polishing of my diamond life and still forthcoming, my God continues to bring forth my spiritual gifts and talents that the brilliance of His glory and power is reflected through. Its unique qualities are as follows: the hardest of all known substances, which only can be cut with another diamond or diamond dust; its name comes from the Greek term "adamas," meaning "unconquerable"; and known for its outstanding brilliance and fire. I'm also reminded through this process that only God can change the heart and mind of man if His will is chosen.

> "And I will give them one heart, and a new spirit I will put within them. I will remove the heart of stone from their flesh and give them a heart of flesh, that they may walk in my statutes and keep my rules and obey them. And they shall be my people, and I will be their God. But as for those whose heart goes after their detestable things and their abominations, I will bring their deeds upon their own heads, declares the Lord God."
> **Ezekiel 11:19-21**

"Who shall separate us from the love of Christ? Shall tribulation, or distress, or persecution, or famine, or nakedness, or danger, or sword? As it is written, "For your sake we are being killed all the day long; we are regarded as sheep to be slaughtered. No, in all these things we are more than conquerors through him who loved us. For I am sure that neither death nor life, nor angels nor rulers, nor things present nor things to come, nor powers, nor height nor depth, nor anything else in all creation, will be able to separate us from the love of God in Christ Jesus our Lord."
Romans 8:35-38

My longing questions, "who am I and why am I here?" is continuously being answered by the polishing of my soul by God wanting its pureness to descend into our material world and demonstrate its power and glory and to illuminate the universe to reflect Him, the Creator of all creation.

Through these refracts, reflects, and disperses of light in our lives, spiritual gifts and talents are refined and brought forth as passions for the up building of God's kingdom here on earth as it is in heaven. The brilliancy of the diamond reflects its passions. The more it fires out light the intensity of passions are deepen and revealed. My first "passionate" identification began in 1994 when I unknowingly started on a quest to know the truth of God by His calling and appointed time. Our immersion in material survival (desiring a good job, nice clothes, home, etc.) makes it difficult for us to recognize the restlessness of our inner being. Our life is preoccupied by work, eating, sleeping, paying bills, and entertaining ourselves.

In August 1997 my preoccupation by work had been altered by God's grace through a tragic accident as stated earlier. Six months prior to the accident, I was led diligently every day to visit with one of our church mothers, Sis. Barbara. She was the oldest teacher for the children. She and I bonded through her granddaughter and my daughter. Our time together became more and more consumed along with my family. She was instantly killed, and I was injured for life (right leg and ankle). Through my recovery journey, God illuminated His Word to me in the knowledge and understanding that a mantle was passed on for me to carry. That mantle was the birthing of Rock of Ages Missionary Baptist Church Children's Church in Belvedere, DE. I loved children but did not have a passion and/or experience in nothing of this nature. BUT GOD, in His infamous power and wisdom just keeps on pouring out His abundant love and grace upon the apple of His eye (mankind). As noted of His abundance, He's continuously polishing the passions of my diamond life in the areas of education (theology, medical, etc.), caregiving (natural and spiritual), teaching, and so many more to come that I've not been introduced to and/or recognize. As stated in 1 Cor 2:6-13,

> "Yet among the mature we do impart wisdom, although it is not a wisdom of this age or of the rulers of this age, who are doomed to pass away. But we impart a secret and hidden wisdom of God, which God decreed before the ages for our glory. None of the rulers of this age understood this, for if they had, they would not have crucified the Lord of glory. But, as it is written,
>
> "What no eye has seen, nor ear heard, nor the heart of

man imagined,
what God has prepared for those who love him" —
these things God has revealed to us through the
Spirit. For the Spirit searches everything, even the
depths of God. For who knows a person's thoughts
except the spirit of that person, which is in him? So
also no one comprehends the thoughts of God except
the Spirit of God. Now we have received not the spirit
of the world, but the Spirit who is from God, that we
might understand the things freely given us by God.
And we impart this in words not taught by human
wisdom but taught by the Spirit, interpreting spiritual
truths to those who are spiritual."

These type facets of passion are only recognized by a
trained eye as we surrender to His will at an appointed time
of polishing.

We are all diamond cutters, but there is only one master
cutter, "Spirit of God", who trains us all in the process. This
step of the process, "poised", is the continuation of growth
and revealing of the many facets that lie within your heart and
mind. Reminder: only a diamond can cut a diamond; and,
only one soul can reach another — "Each One, Reach One with
His Holy Word" — this was our motto at ROAMBC. This can
only be done by the empowerment of the Spirit of God unto
His disciples sharing the brilliance of His grace and love by
faith. Our mission is to recognize that all souls are diamonds
in rough and we are to help actualize every individual's
precious potential by excavating, cutting and polishing and
revealing the brilliance within, allowing every man, woman,
and child's inner personality to emerge and illuminate the
world in which we live for God's glory and power. I was

poised at this appointed time to share "My Diamond Life" with you. The struggle to complete this was undeniably one that one would have given up and quit, but my belief & slogan of life as a Diamond of God: "Quitting is not an Option!"

Sam Jacobson ends this lesson with, "Why did God create diamonds? Perhaps to have an example in our lives of the value and preciousness of the soul; a soul that lies deeply embedded in rock and which, when it emerges, shines with unprecedented brilliance and fire."

There are many tips that you will add to this list as you endure your diamond life – "Polished, Passionate, Poised", but I'm sharing a few from my list:

- Intimate prayer life with God (not just daily but momentarily)

- Seek the truth of God for knowledge, understanding and wisdom of who you are and your purpose—not others. Remember diamonds can only be cut by a diamond or diamond dust. Only God know your heart and mind because He created you in His image and likeness and brought forth His glory in His precious diamond.

- Don't allow people, places, and things to distract you from following the passions that have been given to you by God. He is your Good Shepherd and you shall not want (Psalm 23).

- Remember you are a servant in the capacity of a diamond, shining the brilliance of God's glory to others. There will be trials of life that will strive to distract and detour you off your path but,

"Count it all joy, my brothers, when you meet trials of various kinds, for you know that the testing of your faith produces steadfastness. And let steadfastness have its full effect, that you may be perfect and complete, lacking in nothing. If any of you lacks wisdom, let him ask God, who gives generously to all without reproach, and it will be given him. But let him ask in faith, with no doubting, for the one who doubts is like a wave of the sea that is driven and tossed by the wind. For that person must not suppose that he will receive anything from the Lord; he is a double-minded man, unstable in all his ways."
James 1:2-8

"I appeal to you therefore, brothers, by the mercies of God, to present your bodies as a living sacrifice, holy and acceptable to God, which is your spiritual worship. Do not be conformed to this world, but be transformed by the renewal of your mind, that by testing you may discern what is the will of God, what is good and acceptable and perfect."
Rom 12:1-3

DIAMONDS, you've been "Polished, Passionate, and Poised" for such a time as this to shine the love of God in this dark world! Thank you, Michelle and my dear Sister Co-Authors, in sharing this part of your journey of diamond life with me. Much love & blessings upon you all!!

THE DREAM CATCHER

Lia Abney

Every great dream begins with a dreamer. Always remember, you have within you the strength, the patience, and the passion to reach for the stars to change the world.

~Harriet Tubman

As I look at pictures of my younger self, I see eyes of a girl who lacked certainty of where her life would lead – a dream of her own. Do you remember in primary school having to write an essay to your future self about where you will be in 15 or 20 years? I vaguely remember that I wrote I would be a teacher. Yes, a teacher. *Why?* Because that is what I was told I would be good at by teachers that barely knew me or who I believed really cared about me. But an unfamiliar feeling that I was meant to be more and do more kept haunting me way into my adult life. Yet here I was this little scrawny light skinned girl who did not have a clue where her life would end up was lost in so many ways and without a purpose. It turns out that my whole life was written in this way. Doing what others said I should do rather than following my own path. This led me down a road during the first part of my adult life making decisions that was the easiest rather than taking bold steps that where purposeful without fear. So, here I was entering a world without a guide to lead me – someone to catch me from falling. I felt like the lights had been turned off and I was blindly stumbling through life. This caused me to be restless despite all the years I gave as a professional woman in Corporate America.

Let Your Light Shine

If you would have told me back, then that today I would be a professional businesswoman I am sure I would have found that hard to believe. I did not view myself as a woman that had it together (polished, passionate or poised). I hid in my own thoughts and eventually my emotions controlled my actions which I found myself missing out on God's plans for my life. I allowed my doubts and insecurities to create a mindset of self-doubt that is until the Dream decided to CatcHer (catch her). I gave into the dream that was pulling at my gut. You see nothing but hardship and bad circumstances was the norm for me – *a story I will tell another time*. I didn't have adults or teachers encouraging me to be better or give me hopes of a successful life. I didn't know what success looked like. The troubles I had to endure greatly affected my sense of belonging or seeing what I could accomplish in my future life, You see…unknowingly, I had built up this wall that not only prevented others from getting in but it held me hostage from pursing my destiny mostly out of fear of the unknown. So of course, I would always choose the less costly route. It took for me to get to my lowest point – a marriage that had ended for the second time, no money, and having to build a new home in a city that was unfamiliar to find my true self. *Or at least I thought.* It is so easy to blame others on your troubles, but truth be told most of our troubles is because of the choices we make. I had to make a decision to no longer follow what was expected of me but to boldly and confidently step out and walk in my purpose. This meant that I needed to embrace change and not allow feelings of inadequacy engulfed me because I did not feel polished or significant in my role as a professional black woman, mother, or help mate. I needed to change my thinking and the words I was willing to accept in my atmosphere. No more could I accept anything that was not aligned with what I was believing. I polished my thoughts by posting notes around me as reminders of who I was to be. I checked my own attitude and activated my faith to shine brighter than my circumstances or what others thought or said about me. Yes, I did it. I was not about to wait for somebody to do it for me. Yep, I took the power and dominion to change my direction.

Passion to Dream

The passion within me was screaming to get out. I needed to dream. Are you at that point where you need to dream again? To dream is to see your passion NOW that is to happen in the FUTURE. To dream is to have a PASSION to reach for what you desire to change your life and those around you for good not evil (nothing but faith). Jeremiah 29:11 says it best, *"For I know the plans I have for you," declares the LORD, "plans to prosper you and not to harm you, plans to give you hope and a future."* As I came to understand these biblical words, I became confident in knowing that the trials and tribulations I had endured was part of my journey. Yes, it hurt and yes it was emotionally painful but how amazing it was to know that it was not intentional (not God's divine plan for my life) as I would like to believe and that there was a purpose in my pain. It built up my ability to persevere no matter how hard it got. It made me an overcomer, a conqueror and for the first time I began to believe with ALL MY HEART that I can do ALL things through Christ who STRENGTENS me!

Step in Faith

So, Lia what is your passion? How did you find it? Through self-discovery I've come to fully understand that I have a passion for sharing knowledge and empowering others to pursue their own destiny. I discovered my passion through the struggles I had on my job which would challenge me to think about who I was and what I was meant to be. I no longer allowed my paycheck to define my purpose. Now, please understand that for some of you your purpose is in the workplace, or your community or globally. We sometimes error by not understanding what path we are to take in our journey. Don't abort the process! Our trials allow us to grow and draw closer to God.

As a minority woman in a male dominated field it was challenging to get my foot in the door especially where the work environment was mostly dictated by policy and guidelines and yes, the good old boy system. I'm sure this sounds very familiar for some of you. No matter how much training or education you gained and yes, the countless late hours of worked self-satisfaction eludes us. It became difficult for me after two years of low staffing and mistreatment that I fell into the same trap of following expectations of others rather than stepping out boldly towards my destiny. This was my error in thinking that my responsibility of sticking with it was more beneficial and God gracing me for the struggle. NO, it was by my choice rather than being brave enough to "Step out in Faith". Don't get me wrong I had one foot in my destiny and the other fully planted into what was comfortable – the 9 to 5. I learned and gained useful valuable skills that I could transfer to pursuing the plans God has for me. This was a time for me to hold on to faith and just JUMP (at least according to Steve Harvey). And it is about knowing your season, is it your season?

However, if you are anything like me jumping is not always an option. But this time I needed to JUMP and believe that God had the rest. So, even as I write this in 2020, I am poised to let go of my corporate job to fully pursue what God has designed for me – what I am most passionate about. This did not come without preparation and yes, some apprehension. To be "poised" is to be self-assured or confident. You must be confident in your pursuit of your dreams. Here are a few things to consider as you pursue your dreams:

- **Prayer** - I can't say enough how important prayer is in your transition if you are a person of faith. Prayer allows you to seek wisdom on your circumstances and to clearly hear from God on what actions you should take to prepare yourself. What direction you should go. Whom you should connect. We all have heard at one time or another that God desires to be included in all aspects of our lives. So why leave Him out of this crucial decision in your life? Yes, we want to be assured but remember that if you are "poised" you are confident of your journey. And this happens through prayer.

- **Plan** – Habakkuk 2:2-3 (The Message) states, "And then God answered: "Write this. Write what you see. Write it out in big block letters so that it can be read on the run. This vision-message is a witness pointing to what's coming. It aches for the coming—it can hardly wait! And it doesn't lie. If it seems slow in coming, wait. It's on its way. It will come right on time." A "vision-message" allows you to see where you are going and is a way to communicate to others what you need and defines who you are. Without it there is no identity. There is not a clear picture to guide you in your path. And until it comes you will continue to ache for it. Did you notice that Moses and the people of Israel had a plan – the Ten Commandments? It provided instructions from God to Israel. It communicated God's instructions – a guide to righteousness. And when the people diverted from the vision, they experienced uncomfortable environments. And guess what, that same plan still applies today! My point is that it was written, and it provided clear instructions to Israel to lead God's people to His promises. Write clear instructions for your future! It doesn't need to be perfect. Allow for mistakes and don't be so hard on yourself. Decide what is most beneficial for you not merely what others think is best for you. Do not get lost in the doing. Find yourself in the journey. So, get started today by writing a plan that gives you instructions on where you want to go as professional women that are POLISHED, PASSIONATE, and POISED.

- **Pursue** – DREAM BIGGER, BRIGHTER and then DREAM SOME MORE!! Now, I must express strongly that to pursue something requires an undeniable and unmovable focus. This requires a self-assessment to understand what motivates you. Nobody goes through life with a desire to fail. And I was not immune to those same fears, but I also knew that STOPPING was not an option. Identifying distractions and destructive behavior where key to my growth. It was essential for me to clearly identify barriers in that I CREATED to travel this road designed specifically for me. Yes, I needed to face my own flaws. Facing these flaws in my life was not easy. It requires a strong desire to want more and do something not for self-gratification but for something greater. I had to loudly say to myself "okay Lia, enough is enough, it's time to keep it moving there is no time for this mess". I also needed people around me to not only encourage me but to challenge me to take a good look at myself to address any self-defeating behaviors. I mean who really wants to look at themselves so critically to identify their own weaknesses – *nobody does!* There are enough people hating on you, right – why would I want to take such a critical look at myself. IT IS SO YOU CAN CHANGE THE NARRATIVE OF YOUR LIFE. It is so you can PURSUE destiny. This is about how bad you want to see how far you can go and what you can achieve. It is so that you and I no longer make excuses or ignore our responsibility and role in pursuing destiny. It's never anybody else's job to do it for us. Those that encourage you, mentor you or coach you have their role. Your role is to take what is given to you and walk it out by faith.

37

My journey as an author and speaker did not begin until well into my late 40s. In my mind I could have believed that my late start would be fruitless. I am so glad that my desires outweighed my thoughts. This alone could have caused me to live just an everyday life. Living day by day without a purpose. However, I found comfort in my struggles as God's words provided comfort and direction. Perhaps you are finding yourself struggling to find your true authentic self – your purpose and your vision. How to move from a hot mess to "Polished, Passionate, and Poised". Please be encouraged to keep seeking you will find her, and she will become the "Dream CatcHer".

Sources:

Brainyquote retrieved September 17, 2019 at
https://www.brainyquote.com/topics/passion-quotes

Gateway Bible retrieved September 17, 2019 at
https://www.biblegateway.com/

GREATER IN ME

Ira Warren

A s I rehearsed the title of this anthology "Polished Passionate & Poised over and over in my mind I pictured the deity of God and how infallible He is. A God that created us in his image In Genesis 2:7 then the Lord God formed the man of dust from the ground and breathed into his nostrils the breath of life, and the man became a living creature. My life is not the result of spontaneous reorganization of molecules within his body, nor is it derived by evolution from any animal or evolutionists teaching but a direct gift from God.

A Chinese proverb says, "The gem cannot be polished without friction

I chuckled to myself when I did a brief research on gems. The process of a gem and us are two of the same. Gems are beautiful, and we can all be beautiful like gems. However, let us not forget the process in which a gem becomes and gem. The gem was dug out of the earth rough and dirty. Then the gem is sent to a gem cutter to knock off brittle fractured material, cut, shape, heated then the gem is polished. God does the same with us only if we surrender ourselves to go through the process. One of the most difficult parts as a believer we're not immune to life's trials and tribulations. Honey yes, your faith will be test!

I know, I've questioned many of times why would a loving God allow me/us to go through molestation, the death of a child, diseases, financial hardship, worry and fear? I mean if he loves you/me he would take all these things away that besets us. After all, doesn't loving us mean He wants our lives to be comfortable without struggles? Huh, no, it doesn't!

Romans 8:28amp We are assured and know that (God being a partner) in their labor) all things work together and are (fitting into a plan) for good to and for those who love God and are called according to (His) design and purpose.

Yes, God allows trials and tribulations as a part of our lives. It's all working together for our good and with divine purpose. As in all things, God's ultimate purpose for us is to grow more and more into the image of His Son. This is the goal of the Christian, and everything in life, including the trials and tribulations, is designed to enable us to reach that goal. It is part of the process of sanctification and fitted to live for His glory.

In 1Peter1;6-7 amp 6 (You should) be exceedingly glad on this account though now for a little while you may be distressed by trials and suffer temptation.7 So that (the genuineness) of your faith may be tested, (your faith) which is infinitely more precious than the perishable gold which is tested an purified by fire. (This proving of your faith is intended) to redound to (your) praise and glory and

honor when Jesus Christ (the Messiah, the Anointed One) is revealed.

Trials develop godly character, and that enables us to "rejoice in our sufferings, because we know that suffering produces perseverance, perseverance, character, and character, hope. For one to continue to be polished, Passionate and poised we must not make excuses for our trials and tribulations. Let's not get it twisted we can be our own demise and chose to sin over obedience to Christ. I struggled with fornication for many years. I felt I was justified because I was molested and raped. You see when I ask Christ to come into my life that old Ira was nailed to the cross with Christ. My old sinful self was buried with Christ and raised up by the Father, so was I/You raised up to "walk in newness of life".

You see to understand the new creation, first we must grasp that it is in fact a creation, something created by God. John 1:13 tells us that this new birth was brought about by the will of God. I/You did not inherit the new nature or decide to recreate ourselves anew. Neither did God simply clean up our old nature. He created something entirely fresh and unique. Second," old things have passed away." The "old" refers to everything that is part of our old nature-natural pride, love of sin, reliance on works, and our former opinions, habits and passions. Most significantly, the things we once loved has passed away. Question Have they? Yes, I'm talking about self-love and the self-justification, self-promotion and self-justification that dims our light in Christ. The new creature looks outwardly towards Christ instead of inwardly toward self.

When one has gone through the process of being born again, we do know we have to continue to die to self-daily. Sanctification hit different when we pick up our crosses to follow Christ. That cross is an instrument of death. We lose our wants and desires for God's desires. Dying to self is never portrayed in Scripture as something optional in the Christian life. It is the reality of the new birth, no one can come to Christ unless she/he is willing to see his old life crucified with Christ and begin to live anew in obedience to Him. I praise God for all that has happened in my life. Yes, even the ugly. The molestation, the rapes, being homeless and washing up in gas stations and scraping up change to buy a 99-cent sandwich. God was in the mist of it all.

He's grace was and is enough for every moment of every day of my life. IAM SET APART>

In Jeremiah 18 The word that came to Jeremiah from the Lord;2 Arise, and go down to the potter's house, and there I will let you hear my words. "3 So I went down to the potters' house, and there he was working at his wheel. 4 And the vessel he was making of clay was spoiled in the potter's hand, and he reworked it into another vessel, as it seemed good to the potter to do.

God sees the blemishes in the clay (us). God then reshapes us with purpose in mind. We must die to our will and desire and be pliable to the hands of the Father so that he can shape and mold us. I resisted God's breaking in my life many times. I thought I knew what was best for my life. I dimed my light by my plans, my pride, and my way. I had the attitude God's plan wasn't happening on my time or fast enough. Yeah, I know I'm a sinner saved by grace through faith. Yeah, I accepted you as my Lord and Savior, but can we do this and that my way? God made it clear at that moment He will not share his glory with no man. Like my granny use to say, "you betta eat lots of humble pie when you running this race as a child of God."

Isaiah 42:8 "I am the Lord, that is My Name; My glory I will not give another, Nor My praise to carved idols.

I dimed my own light by placing demands on God. I was chasing the after physical pleasure and selfish gain. I knew I was commanded to live a different way to "put on the Lord Jesus Christ, and make no provision for the flesh, to gratify my desires" (Romans 13:14) My positioning was all wrong. I was saying to God, "I'm more important than you." Ouch! what was I thinking? I realize I was believing lies from my own beliefs and the adversary who is the father of lies. Here is some of the lies I began to tell myself. "God isn't concern with what I do.", The fruit in my life is from my own labor, my comfort is more important than others. I was full of myself. This is called living a lie and the truth isn't in you.

I was broken and felt inadequate and unworthy of God's grace. I had to understand that He was that greater in me not me greater in him. God is more majestic that my mind will ever be able to comprehend. Yet, he is intricately concerned with every aspect of my life. When God says he chastens those whom he loves. Get ready! You will have a choice to repent or go on with your life. Pride can override the truth and cause one to view God as low on your list. This is what John says, "He must increase, but I must decrease." (John 3;30). My position after Christ is all of grace. What I deserve is infinitely worse than what I've been given. I was dead in my trespasses.

I was helpless and hopeless. Living according to the world standards, following Satan, and living to satisfy my own desires. I was literally scorning the grace of God with my pride. My position has changed. I have surrendered my life fully to God. Yes, this process of following Christ is painful. I had to understand this walk isn't about me and my self-love and my desires.

This is the command that Paul gave in Philippians 2. 'Do nothing out of selfish ambition or conceit, but in humility consider other a more important than yourselves." I'm no more valuable than anyone else. I don't deserve more grace than the next person. If I thought I was better than the next person or deserve more grace than the next person, it would be a contradictory to the nature of grace. It is a gift that is given to me and you that we don't deserve. To be Polished Passionate & Poised I continuously must look at humility Christ set for me to practices. Het emptied himself by assuming the form of a servant, taking on the likeness of humanity. And when he had come as a man, he humbled himself by becoming obedient to the point of death- even to death on a cross.

God's will be for me and you to be holy just s He is holy. His desire is my sanctification. God is sovereign to bring that holiness to fruition. I depend on the Holy Spirit to help me stay humble. And not have my own trinity of me, myself and I. Matthew 5:16amp Let your light shine before men such a way that they may see your good deeds and moral excellence, and (recognize and honor and) glorify your father who is in heaven. There is a song by JJ Weeks Band called Let Them See You. What JJ Weeks is saying strip me of self and let man only see you in me.

One verse says Who am I without your praise Another smile, Another face Another Breath, A grain of sand, passing quickly though your hands, I give my life, an offering, Take it all take everything
Hook: Let them see you, in me, Let them hear you when I speak, let them feel you, when I Sing Let them see you in me.

I don't want to be Polished Passionate & Poised for self by for Christ and for others to see Christ in me. I know I must continue to die daily to self and my wants and needs. Praising God, praying and reading His word. This beautiful love letter that so rich with truth and promises for those who are obedient to His word. Going through the process of being broken and shaped is all for the Glory of God. The awesome part is we reap the benefits of walking in obedience.

Psalm 139:14 I praise you because I am fearfully and wonderful made; your works are wonderful; I know that full well.

God made all the delicate, inner parts of my body. He knit me together within my mothers' womb. I was made wonderfully complex. God knew me as he was painstakingly designing me with much loving care. I didn't just evolve into what I am. I was created and designed with a purpose. And the blueprint of me are like other human beings but they're not the same. Am unique- and so are you.

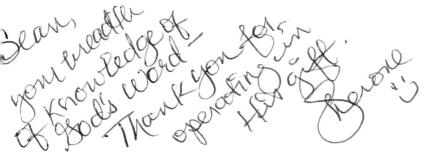

THE THREE P'S: STORY TIME

Sherone Weeks

Dedication: to my Mother, Sharon Elizabeth Tilghman Weeks aka Pokie (1957-2011). You taught me to be brave, unashamed and you showed me how to love the Lord. Although I didn't know you would leave us so soon, you left a wealth of knowledge that I use daily. I hope that you're proud of us, we think and talk about you often. Thanks *Ma*, you were the evolution of Psalm 31, a Virtuous Woman.

I enjoy telling stories...and listening to others tell their stories! Although I often get sidetracked and have side stories within the original story, I'm told that my stories are comical and energetic. The art of storytelling, I believe, is essential in preserving heritage and a means of continuing a family's identity. Our life experiences, whether awful or delightful, create stories that we can't help but share, with our friends and loved ones.

Many of our *unfavorable* stories, that come from distressing experiences, challenge us and increase our capacity strength for future experiences and to share with others during their times of need. Neitzsche is credited with saying "That which does not kill us makes us stronger. "said it best, I couldn't have imagined that my Mother would pass away, suddenly, at 54 years of age. Although I miss her daily, I am grateful for all that she instilled in me, and that I can impart her life altering principles into my children. I'm also grateful that my children were close to my Mother, who they affectionately called "Mom-momPokie", spending time with her and creating their own memories of her. (Of course, there's a whole separate story about how she came to be called "Pokie", which I'll share at another time.) My children often share their fond memories of *Pokie*, our frequent trips to Wal-Mart and her joyful habit of bursting into song at a moment notice-often in the middle of a conversation.

Growing up with my sister Sheraya, influenced by our grandparents, aunts, uncles and friends of the family, there was always the opportunity for a story. Versions of the story told and retold, for entertainment, to clarify details since the last time it was recited or to offer a life lesson to the younger family members (my sister, myself and our cousin Jabari). I looked forward to holidays and special occasions, because I knew there would be stories-old and new, to hear, to recite along with the teller, to laugh at and to inadvertently memorize. My family was "old school", in that children weren't allowed to engage in the stories. The children in the family were to "be seen and not heard" and to "stay out of grown folks business". Most of the stories that I heard as a child, I've passed on to my children, with hopes that they'll value the experience behind the stories and one day, share the stories with their children. Stories like how my Mother had driver's education in school, with a teacher named Mr. Beebee, who slept during the driving lessons but all the students managed to pass the driving test. I've never met Mr. Beebee, but I wonder if he snored during the driving lessons,

48

or which make and model 1970-something car that they drove for the lessons.

As a Mother of four wonderful the relevance of sharing stories, experiences and life challenges with our children, can help them cope when life comes at them. We share, with the hopes that they won't repeat our "mistakes" or experience the hurt. Even in our mistakes, our purpose can be fulfilled if we believe the sacred text that declares "we can be so sure that every detail in our lives of love for God is worked into something good".

In the tradition of a good ole Hayman/Tilghman story-telling occasion, this chapter will share the *Three P's*, connected to one of my cherished family members.

Polished-refined, sophisticated or elegant

Virgie Gertrude Hayman Tilghman, my Mother's mother, was all of 5'5" with a petit but sturdy frame and a face the shown lines of hard work and worry. She was the "church Mother" at the Apostolic church that we attended almost every day of the week. She could clap on beat to the congregational hymn *and* give you a stern reprimand-if you were misbehaving during service. My sister and I went to live with our grandparents when my mother had a stroke at age 29, in 1986. Robert (aka pop pop) and Virgie (aka mom mom) lived in an old country house on an old country road in Caroline County, Maryland. Going to "the country" to visit Mom-mom and Pop-pop, was like an adventure; a sharp contrast from where we lived in Alexandria, VA.

Among the many treasures at Mom-mom and Pop-pop's house, was a frequently polished (rarely used) dining room set that showcased a wooden 6-foot table, six matching chairs, a buffet that sat along the far wall and the infamous china cabinet that seemed to stand at attention in the corner of the dining room. These furnishings appeared monstrous as if they came alive at night, but during the day, storied items that we as children weren't allowed to touch. The china cabinet is now housed in my dining area, storing items that *my* children aren't allowed to touch! The hutch and china cabinet were home to unique dishes, different color glass containers, Corning ware, and real Silverware. I didn't understand the value of these pieces as a child, but I did understand those pieces were sacred and were handled delicately. In the hutch, next to the silverware, was a bottle of *TarnX* silver polish. Before special occasions, I watched my grandfather prepare the Silverware that would be used by our guests. He couldn't directly handle the polish with his bare hands, so he wore gloves to protect his hands. He didn't use just any old piece of material to polish the silver, there was a special polishing cloth used to preserve those cherished items.

The care that my grandparents took of each of the objects in their dining room, showed me the importance of being polished. The sacred text declares that we are *fearfully and wonderfully made*. Therefore, we too must be polished, to sustain ourselves along this journey we call life. There are times when we are "stored" and times when we are on display for all to see. There are seasons and special occasions when we are shown off and other times that we focus on home and concerns of the family. As we move through life's seasons, be mindful to take inventory of our whole well-being; and to polish when needed.

Passionate-showing or caused by strong feelings or a strong belief

Virgie Christine Tilghman also known as "Ant Teeny", is a *Professional Shade Thrower*. Well-traveled, well-seasoned, and tenacious, she doesn't back down easily. If I published a dictionary, the definition of <u>passionate</u> would have a picture of my Aunt Teeny. Growing up in the 60's she has an innate, raw edge. You just can't tell Aunt Teeny any ole thing, life experience has taught her different.

As teenagers, my sister and I would visit our aunt during the Summer "vacations"; she lived in Silver Spring, MD. This was a treat to us, and we looked forward to what the Summer would bring. Escaping from the slow country life, to the fast-paced city life of public transportation, community recreation centers and fun to be had, within walking distance. We made friends that we could hang out with each day, often getting into senseless mischief. Friends that we keep in touch with today, mostly by way of social media. We knew the unwritten rules before visiting, but we always seemed to ignore them.

- Don't go in her bedroom while she's at work.

- Don't have anyone in the house while she's at work.

- Don't go into anyone else's house.

- Don't eat up all the food; grocery shopping was only done every other Friday, at the local *Giant Food store*.

- Don't go anywhere outside of the community development, without calling her at work to ask first.

So, when Aunt Teeny's valued marble chess set was broken (while we had friends in the house and when she was at work), Sheraya and I had to take the blame! With fear and trembling, we created a story of how we were running through the house and I accidently knocked it over. First, there's no running in the house; secondly, she knows we weren't that careless. That's the story we stuck with, until this manuscript is published! Aunt Teeny's quaint suburban townhouse was like a museum; filled with genuine artistry that she'd collected during her travels to several countries of the continent of Africa.

I've watched Aunt Teeny successfully manage community organizations, giving detail to every administrative function, whether serving a dozen or serving hundreds. She's an advocate for the aging population, helping them maintain their independence at home, enjoying their lives although the days are few. More than anything, I wonder what life experiences are behind that fire in her eyes! How did she come to love being *Black and proud* and all things about the Black culture? When did she purchase her first painting by a Black artist, or an African inspired wooden wall hanging for her apartment?

Growing up, I thought Aunt Teeny had a hypervigilant attitude and disposition. Listening to Aunt Teeny and her friends' stories about "the good ole days", seemed so far-fetched from my 90's Hip hop influence. I now see that the same social climate of the 60's is in the 21st century, slowing being undisguised and strategically dismantled. Her view of social injustice: German Shepherd attack dogs and fire hydrants opened on peaceful protesters. My first view of injustice, 1991, when Rodney King was violently beaten by police officers. Two generations influenced to passionately become community agents of change.

What drives the human psyche to work to discover the destiny of that individual? Does passion come naturally? What is the "why" that motivates an individual? Is it nature or nurture, or a combination of both? Is it our spiritual being that yearns to find what God created us for? That teacher who told us they believed in us and we can do great things! Or maybe it's from a place of hurt and pain, that made you vow no one would endure what you went through. So, you became passionate, and an advocate for others who experience similar adversity. Our passion becomes the vice by which we create change, within ourselves, our families, our neighborhood, the workplace, the meso and macro levels of society.

Poised- having a graceful and elegant bearing

Ethel Marie Tilghman (1945-2003), was a lady of dignity and fortitude, who I consider to be the epitome of *poised*. From her manicured nails to her delicate smile and coiffed hairdo, she proudly maintained an *elegant bearing*. When my sister and I were in her presence, we knew the rehearsed rules of etiquette; to sit with our legs closed, chew with our mouths closed, and to carry ourselves like a ladies. When we visited Aunt Ethel for the weekend, we knew that Saturday would be full of "running errands"; from Woodward & Lothrop, to People's Drugstore and if time allowed, to J.C. Penny's. In order to be prepared for Sunday service at Greater Morning Star, there was an early Saturday hair appointment with Ms. Mills, identical dresses to be ironed, unscuffed patent leather shoes, matching purses (with tissues, a $1 or $2, and hand lotion) and fresh new stockings that completed the outfit. Aunt Ethel had no children of her own, but she spoiled her godchildren, and her two favorite nieces, teaching us the essentials of becoming a lady.

Aunt Ethel was a legal professional who lived in an exquisite apartment rise in Washington, D.C., minutes from the White House. During the workweek, she could be found on the subway platform, among the droves of other commuters on their way to the business arena of the District. Like the other professional women in their Ann Taylor suits, carrying designer bags and briefcases with important documents, she took pride in her occupation and her outward appearance. She wore tennis shoes to work, carrying an additional bag with her Etienne Aigner high heeled pumps to change into. Aunt Ethel *stayed* sharp! She always seemed so unbothered by what was going on around her; whether in the Nation's Capital or at our family reunion. *Minding our own business* was always the task of the day; staying mindful of every detail of our own disposition.

Virgie, Ethel, Teeny, and Sharon didn't just talk, they showed us the value of being young ladies. My sister and I didn't value those lessons as silly teenagers, feeling like they were always "picking on us" and there were "too many rules". Now raising our own children, we both recognize what they were trying to engrain in us about how to handle ourselves, *gracefully and with an elegant bearing*. Having three beautiful, peculiar and ambitious daughters, I certainly value the art of teaching them how to flourish, in becoming polished, passionate and poised.

Grateful for an upbringing among women of virtue and strength, I am humbled to share these stories in their honor. Continued peace and blessings to every reader.

POISED BY GRACE

Linette Michelle Howard

So, there I was, fired at fifty. After 8 years and 10 months of working for this organization, they job fired me. It actually wasn't much of a surprise though to me, as they had been trying to find a reason to fire me for years, but for some reason, they could never seem to make up something good enough to nail me for, until now and even this reason was poorly made up and underneath an undeniable pile of hate, but here we go…

I had often wondered why God would allow for me to go through such a hellish time and for what would seem like forever, I realize now that I was being polished and shaped, God was molding me into more of his masterpiece, so when it came time for me to share with the world, all of his love and all of his mercy, I would be Poised by his grace.

During the close to 9 years though, that I was with this organization, I was plagued almost daily with what seemed like endless amounts of doubts and fears, loneliness and sadness, despair and hopelessness, brokenness and suicidal thoughts, my job had then turned up the heat, they had begun to treat me so unfairly, that I had begun to think that God had forsaken me, and that he just didn't care about me anymore. I even remember one time crying out to him saying, "Father, where are you? Don't you see what they're doing to me, do you even care"? And I just cried...

Day after day, and month after month and year after year, I was overlooked, overworked and underpaid and made to feel invisible, like I didn't have a voice... But I wasn't invisible and I did have a voice, because every morning when I looked in the mirror, I saw myself and I told myself that I was powerful and that I was beautiful and that I was unbreakable, a masterpiece that God had created, so no matter what they did or what they said, it would never break me down, it would only make me better, because I was being Poised by his grace.

Didn't they know who I was, and didn't they know who my father was? Apparently not, because they never stopped trying to break me down, still... I'm not sure what happened but, it was as if God had said "ENOUGH" and then all of a sudden, after crying and praying endlessly and hearing nothing from God for a long time, he then said to me " all of these things that are happening, they are happening for you NOT to you! I know that you are hurting right now, and it seems like the enemy is winning, but he is not, and he will not". And so, I started to cheer up and God started sending me angels (in human form) to help me and inspirations to get me through the day and his Holy Spirit started to comfort me more. So no matter how bad things got at work, at home and in my business, I kept praying and I kept seeking God and his infinite wisdom, so that I might get a better understanding of what I should be gaining from all of this torment and also pleading with God to renew and increase my faith every single day, because unfortunately, I had let what I was seeing, make me doubt what I knew. And after some time went by, I started trusting in God more and more every day and the doubts of him not caring about what was happening to me somewhat diminished. I started going to work with a little more kingdom in my step every day and a smile on my face, realizing that it was only by his grace that I was still there, that he had kept me and was still keeping me from losing my mind and my job. I had also realized that although I was in the fire, God controlled the heat and that I would come out of this fire unharmed by the flames that was all around me and without even the smell of smoke on me!

Still, it would take days, weeks, months and even years for them to fire me, so in the meantime I had to keep finding ways to keep my mind off of how depressed I was inside and how defeated I felt, my job had started recruiting more people to hate me, even the new people that didn't even know me, didn't like me! How degrading was it for me to be and stay on a job that clearly did not want me there. Hell, they had shown it in every way humanly possible, by the unwarranted write ups, the poorly submitted annual reviews of me, the denials for a well-deserved company policy sabbatical, which was granted to everyone except for me.

Again, I went back to God, because clearly, he doesn't want me to stay here, especially not while I'm being mistreated like this, this is crazy, who would stay here? But God said "do not leave, I am preparing a table before you, in the presence of your enemies and in the end, your cup will runneth over", but so in my childlike mind and because everything around me was falling apart, I was like "what table God" these people are winning this battle that you said that you would fight for me! I'm stressed out, I'm over worked, I'm underpaid, they won't promote me, they won't pay for any sort of professional development and they've increased in numbers, meaning that, there are more of them now! And should I mention again that, I am fifty years old now and I've been here for 9 years!

God started then preparing me for the inevitable, I would be fired and although I had wrestled tirelessly with him about this unfair decision, especially since I hadn't done anything wrong, it was going to happen and I had no choice but to trust him. So the day finally came when HR comes to my desk, on a day when she would normally pretend to be working from home and asks if she can speak to me in her office, where I would then join my brand new supervisor, already sitting at the table. "So was this the table that God had been talking about", that he was preparing before me, in the presence of my enemies, because it sure didn't feel like it. So I sit down with a great big smile on my face and then HR says to me "unfortunately Linette this won't be a good meeting" and then I say "Oh I'm sure it will be for me", she then proceeded to tell me how they've decided to practice their "at will termination" rights and that I am being let go. So it was happening, it had in fact just happened and for no apparent reason at all, I had succeeded every yearly performance review with a satisfactory score, challenged every write up as warranted and without true merit, although they would never assent to that, because after all they were building a case against me and needed these write ups in my personnel file, otherwise there were no reprimands and no counseling's, I was great at my job and for the most part, I got along with most of my co-workers. So, what really were they terminating me for, because I wasn't a team player? Nah, well actually yes, because I've never been one for work politics and or brown nosing my boss or anyone in higher positions, I've always believed that, as long as I went to work and did my job with

60

excellence, then why would I then also need to brown nose anyone. The truth is, they fired me because they didn't like me, and not because of anything that I had to them, because remember what I told you, this was a new crew, so they didn't even really know me, but they knew that I was different, and that I was not like them and I don't mean just in the color of my skin, I mean everything about me was in complete contrast to everything they stood for or even knew about me for that matter.

The next few days were a fog, I was numb and still in disbelief that it all had finally happened, and where was God, I needed him now more than ever before, because I had just turned fifty and I didn't have a job, how would I tell my husband, how could I lay such a burden on him like this, how would I take care of my family. I needed to cry, but I was too angry, I needed to pray but I felt like, what would be the use, God isn't listening anyway. So days would go by, and I would wake up with what seemed like the same heartache that I had felt before, back in the day during the times when I was unmarried and single and I would breakup with a boyfriend and every time it would seem like my heart had physically broken itself into pieces and the pain of it all was just too insufferable to carry and then reality finally set in, I didn't have a job and I had suffered through all of that torment for nothing. I was tired of praying, God wasn't listening anyway, but then this voice kept saying to me "God didn't bring you this far to leave you now". Yes, you are fifty and yes, they did fire you, but this is only the beginning, everything that I promised you will come to pass. You have to trust me.

So as I sit here writing my chapter in this book, Polished, Passionate & Poised I cannot describe to you the joy that races through my heart right now, the passion I feel for Christ in my soul right now, the gratefulness I feel to God right now for having come out of that fire, all shiny and brand new, ready to take on the world and tell everyone about the mercies of Jesus Christ.

I wish that I could tell you that some great big miracle happened since then and now all of those people who mistreated me for all of those years, now work for me and I have to now be like Joseph was in Genesis after his brothers had sold him into slavery and he then had to suffer through injustice after injustice, only to meet face to face with them later on, only now he was the Prime Minister of Egypt. I wish that I could tell you that I have this awesome new job, earning 8 figures a month, and I am the happiest that I've ever been, wouldn't that be a miracle. Well, although I'm not earning 8 figures yet and I'm not in a position yet where I have to be good to those people who mistreated me yet, God has been preparing me for the day that I will have to be good to those people, you see all of this time I thought that this was about me, but this was never about me, this was always about God and his purpose and plan for me.

What the enemy meant for evil, God has worked it out for my good!

You see all that torment from my enemies only moved me closer to God and it kept me on my knees in prayer. And now I am fifty years old, more beautiful and more powerful than ever before and Beloved, I am here now to spread the gospel of Jesus Christ. I am Polished, Passionate and Poised by Grace.

Linette Michelle Howard

Acknowledgements

To my lawfully wedded Husband, Leonard William Howard. On June 19th, 2015, I vowed before God and you that I would always have you and hold you, from that day forward, for better or for worse, for richer or for poorer, in sickness and in health, until death do us part. Thank you Mr. Howard for always being my very best friend, thank you for always protecting me, and sometimes even from myself, thank you for praying for me and for us, thank you for being the greatest dad in the whole wide world to your children and last but certainly not the least, thank you for bringing into being the name of my chapter in this book collaboration, Poised by Grace.

I Love You.

HIDDEN WITHIN... WHEN I STUMBLED UPON MYSELF, I FOUND MY PASSION

Robin M. Sample

So many times, I fell. It Was When I Got Up That I Found Myself and My Purpose! Where does my *passion* lie? I asked myself that question several times throughout my life, especially when I was in the process of coming out of the world and trying to find God and myself. What is my *purpose*? For many years, I had no idea what my purpose was. I felt like I was floating through life, not really belonging to anything or anyone, I was just here. But why? Had God made a mistake when He made me? For many years, I believed that He had, but as I matured and grew in Christ, I learned that He made no mistakes, so I was here on *purpose* for a *purpose*. But what was my *purpose*? *Poised*. Now, that was a word that I didn't think would ever be associated with my name. I laugh at my ignorance to the meaning of this word, because when I was younger, perhaps in my early to mid-20's, I thought to be *poised* was to walk with a certain sashay, or swagger. That, I had down pat, LOL, so I thought, because the swing on my back porch told me that I was *poised*. Thank God that little girl grew up, because had she not, and continued to maintain that same ignorant mindset, only God knows what would have become of her. So, today, many years older, much wiser, more mature and focused on God and His plans for her life, that little girl grew up to be *Passionate, Purposed* and *Poised*. That little girl is me. I am her; she is me!

I have worked in the Human Services field for several years. From Psychiatric Rehabilitation Services, to Mental Health Services, to Addictions Counseling, to Domestic Violence Advocacy and Counseling Services, to Sexual Assault and Trauma Advocacy and Counseling Services, back to Domestic Violence Advocacy and Counseling Services, to having four (4) books published, with two (2) more on the way to being published, to motivational speaking, to being featured in the 'She Wins' Domestic Violence Survivor Story Documentary, to recently finishing my Master Degree in Social Work Program Magna Cum Laude, I would like to think that I have finally found my *Passion*, my *Purpose* and I am *Poised* as I walk in my destiny!

It was 20+ years ago when I experienced my first Domestic Violence incident. Of course, I didn't know then that it was DV. I attributed it to my, then, boyfriend, loving me so much that he didn't want anyone else, men that is, to talk to me, be around me or like me, so he beat me up when he saw me talking to another man. I didn't leave him following that incident, although looking back in hindsight, I should have. Little did I know then, it would only get worse, and it did. Much worse. That incident would be the first of many more to come.

As years passed, I found myself in another DV situation, and another, and another. I began to wonder if I had a magnet or a sign on my back that attracted violent men to me because there were very few that I dated who weren't violent. And the funny thing about that is, although I enjoyed spending time with the non-violent ones, I found them to be rather boring, and I always found my way back to the 'bad boys', the violent ones. I don't know why, but I have always been attracted to those type, yet, I don't like their actions, their behaviors, and most of all, I don't like the way they treat me. It was a vicious cycle, one I could never seem to break, which brought me to this simple conclusion; the problem wasn't them; it was ME!

For years, I pointed the finger at every abusive man that came into my life, pointing out their character flaws and defects and telling them everything I saw wrong with them, when in actuality, I should have been pointing that finger at myself, because I was the one who was flawed. Yes, every one of those men was abusive; however, I learned over the years that we teach people how to treat us, and people can only do to us what we allow them to do, and I allowed that maladaptive pattern of behavior from each one of those men, over and over again.

What was wrong with me? Why did I allow those men to abuse me? And the abuse was not only physical, it was also verbal, emotional, mental, psychological, sexual, and spiritual. It wasn't that I thought this type of behavior was okay because I didn't think that all. I knew it was

wrong, I just didn't know how to stop it. I can't recall the exact day that I decided to begin the 'stopping' process of the cycle of abuse in my life, but I do remember that a shift had taken place in my thought process. I became more focused on myself and my children and our well-being and in such, I began looking at going back to school to further my education so that I could get a better job, a job that would be a gateway to a career. I took that first step and I never looked back. I didn't know what life was going to be like in the absence of the tumultuousness of violent/abusive relationships, but once I got a taste of a different lifestyle, I liked it; no, I loved it, and I was determined to never turn back. I remember facilitating a group counseling session when I was an addictions counselor and one of my clients told me I was nothing more than a 'textbook counselor', accusing me of pretending to understand the struggles of an addict when I hadn't experienced addiction for myself. That statement caused something to stir up inside of me and that would mark the first time I would share my experience of addiction with my clients. And it was at that moment that I began to stumble upon my *passion*. That group session would be the beginning of many more of its kind, as more of my clients became interested in learning, not only about my addiction, but also how I had overcome it, and how I came to be an addictions counselor. I had always felt that I had a story to tell due to the many trials, tribulations, and storms that I had endured throughout my life and I had often times dreamed about traveling the world as a motivational speaker, helping to ignite change in the lives of people who, like myself, had suffered a great deal of hurt, pain and trauma. The same way my clients were curious about my history of addiction and how I got to the point in my life where it was all behind me, I had the same curiosity about them. In the weeks to come, I found a common denominator among myself and my clients, and that was pain. Regardless of our substance of choice, the quantity we used, who we used with, where we used, or what type of effect it had had on our lives, we had all suffered a great deal of pain during our lives. What I also learned that I had in common with my clients was that our substances served as a numbing agent or a source of self-medicating. This realization got me to thinking about the huge number of people who had experienced pain and trauma during their lives, especially during childhood, and were still feeling the effects from it during adulthood. My next stop after I left addictions counseling was the job I currently have, which is advocating for victims of Domestic Violence, Sexual Assault, and Trauma. I think it's not by accident that I landed in this position because when I look back over my life, and reflect on all of the jobs I have held, they are each connected to a season in my life when I was experiencing the very struggle(s) that I was tasked to help others break free from. This realization allowed me to conclude that God has been using me long before I realized it.

I struggled with depression and anxiety for years, I struggled with an addiction to alcohol for years, I experienced Domestic Violence throughout most of my life and I was the victim of two (2) Sexual Assaults at an early age, all of which resulted in me having been diagnosed with Posttraumatic Stress Disorder (PTSD) when I was in my early 30s. While I was navigating my way through the traumatic journey called my life, stumbling, falling, getting bumped, bruised and knocked down time after time, little did I know, God was preparing me for, yet, another journey, the 'Post Trauma Journey', where he would use me to share my story of having transitioned from 'Victim' to 'Victorious' to help others find strength and have faith during their own times of struggle and storms. It took me a while to realize what God was doing, hence my first book, 'When I Stopped Being Angry With God', in which I talk extensively about my anger towards God for having allowed me to suffer the way I had, not realizing then that He had a plan for my life all along; I just didn't know it. Isn't it amazing how God works in our lives, blessing us, protecting us, loving us and keeping us in His loving care and we often don't even realize it? I shared all of that to share this. I am very *Passionate* about the work I do today, and as a matter of fact, it's not really work, because even if I wasn't getting paid, I would still do it, so it's much more than a job for me, it's my true *Passion*. I know I can't save everybody I come in contact with who has experienced Addiction issues, Mental Health issues, Domestic Violence, Sexual Assault or any other form of Trauma; however, if I am able to share my story, my testimony with them, it is my prayer that I have at least planted the seed of hope to help them keep going and trusting God because if He delivered me from such hurt, pain and suffering, He will surely do the same thing for them. For many years, I had no idea what my *Purpose* was. I didn't think I had one. I felt like I was just here, drifting through life, not really knowing where I would end up. The best word I can use to describe how I felt is 'Empty'. Then it happened. My client, with his reference of my having been a 'textbook counselor' caused my entire mindset to shift and from that moment forward, I was clear on what my *Purpose* was, and I have been living in it ever since. To help others heal. I can recall a time when I was so unsure of myself that I was afraid to walk into a crowded room for fear of how people would look at me and what they would say about me. I would be so nervous that I would feel my skin getting hot, my stomach would get upset and I felt like my legs were going to crumble beneath me. But now, I confidently walk into crowded rooms *Poised*, with my head held high, feeling sure of myself and knowing that, finally, I am walking in my *Purpose,* full of *Passion*, answering the call that God has on my life. I may not have understood the 'What', 'Why' or 'How' way back when,

70

but I certainly understand now. My *Purpose* lead to my *Passion,* which lead to my transformation from a fearful, insecure little girl, into a *Poised* and Confident Woman; a Woman who is *Passionate, Purposed* and *Poised*!

Meet the
Author Visionary & Co-Authors

Michelle Boulden Hammond

AUTHOR/LIFE COACH/MOTIVATIONAL SPEAKER/ PSALMIST

Creating a Revolution of Inspiration

Michelle Boulden Hammond is a multitalented woman that handles her faith, marriage, business and professional relationships with the power of inspirations. A small town country girl from Talbot County, MD who has risen above life challenges from birth defect to low self esteem, rejection and mental abuse.

She received her Masters of Arts in Human Services in Counseling from Liberty University and holds CLC Certificate from International Coaching Federation. Michelle with her charismatic personality has the power that gives individuals influence to move beyond their now. In her book called Seize the Moment A Moment To Inspire which was released October 2017 takes individuals on a 30 day affirmation and meditation journey that is life changing,

Michelle also is a member of the BSN Black Speakers Network and in this capacity she has hosted and traveled nationally and internationally for women empowerment conferences. In October 2018 she launched a group called TEAM M. A. B. B. (Mind , Affirmations, Beauty & Boldness). This group featured 4 amazing ladies along with Michelle from the arenas of fashion, beauty and mental wellness. TEAM MABB will be conducting tours this coming year. Michelle's hosted Warm Your Heart, Warm Your Mind , Warm Your Soul which is a spiritual awakening women's empowerment retreat for mind , body and soul will be celebrating its 10th year.

Testimonial "My first time at #WHWMWS Michelle's retreat ... I discovered who I really Am... Her motivational talk session called My Life Evaluator was great.

~Judith~

In Facebook Live Social Media she has now opened her platform of IAM2Inspire TV which features weekly at 7pm Tuesdays weekly.

She has received various awards for her community service and humanitarian efforts. In 2016 she was the first African American female in Talbot County,MD to open wellness center. 2016 Dorothy Black Community Service Award through Talbot County NAACP Branch.

Topics

❖ Personal Growth & Development

❖ Life Skills

❖ Holistic Health / Electromagnetic Therapy

❖ Stress Management

Featured on

❖ Ddtalks Radio Show WBGR NETWORK

❖ Women of Distinction Magazine

❖ Co- Author of The Face of Adversity

❖ MCTV

❖ Forgiveness Nation

Website www.moment2inspire.com

Booking information or contact to have TEAM MABB featured in your city 410-253-6937 Email beinspired70@yahoo.com

Royshonda Boulden

Royshonda D. Boulden was born in Easton Maryland, to Royce L. Boulden and Darcel D. Batson, as well as her "Village" of family and friends, who helped mold her into who she is today. Royshonda is currently obtaining her bachelor's in social work at Bowie State University and is a graduate of Chesapeake College, where she obtained her degree in Liberal Arts and Sciences. She currently works as a Victim Advocate for sexual assault victims and part-time with adults with developmental disabilities.

During her years of high school, she began to have an interest in writing. Her start began as she wrote poems and also enrolling in Drama class during her sophomore year.

When describing who she is as a person, Royshonda would consider herself a " big ball of energy", as she aims to help others, making them laugh or being her fun-loving self. In her free time, she loves to write, dance, be creative (crafts), traveling and spending time with family and friends.

Cherry Moaney

Cherry Moaney is a proud mother of 2 and a doting grandmother of one granddaughter, who adds joy to her life. She was born and raised in the small town of Easton, Maryland. She has always had a connection to young people and her desire is to help them become all they aspire to be. She wants young people to realize that there are no limits to what they can do with God's help. She is a woman that has overcome lots of adversities in her life and feels it is now time to share her testimony.

Cherry loves helping people. By day she brings managerial experience and support to a juvenile detention center and at night she helps those that cannot speak English by being an

English as a Second Language instructor. God-fearing, compassionate, superwoman, Cherry enjoys spending time with her children and family and above all serving God.

Sharon R. Cooper Mizell

Sharon R Cooper Mizell is a mother to her disabled veteran daughter, Psychia. She currently serves as a Certified Home Instead Caregiver while through the leading of her Lord Jesus Christ into a season of entrepreneurial ship.

From Palm Sunday 1995, the seasons of her life began to reveal through the acceptance to her call to life eternity with Christ, a life threatening tragic accident in 1997, an extensive care (15+ yrs.) to her husband (veteran) until November 2015, acceptance to the call to ministry in January 2007, ordained on June 2013, became a Certified Caregiver on November 2016 receiving Caregiver of the Year 2017, and received her

Doctorate of Theology in June 2017. Her passion for serving and giving back to others continues her life's journey.

The endurance and perseverance of her journey through Christ has given her an appreciation to her favorite words "Enjoying My Journey"!

August 30, 2019

Lia Abney

Ms. Lia Abney is a veteran with over 25 years of government service managing multimillion dollar projects as a Management Analyst. She is a subject matter expert in strategic planning and business processes management. She continues to stay relevant in her field as she pursues her doctorate degree with Capella University in Public Administration with an emphasis in Leadership.

Ms. Abney is a self published author of Building People Building Kingdoms: The Business Plan and Amazon Best Seller co-author of "Perfectly Imperfect: See Yourself Through the Eyes of God". She is also a contributing author of the first academic book that focus on women civil servants, leaders in Women in Public Administration: Theory and Practice.

Ms. Abney is the owner of Lia Abney, LLC consulting services and is an advocate for women business professionals by connecting them with the right resources to #keepitmoving to provide relevant services to their community and nationally. Lia Abney has been a featured guest speaker on multiple radio, podcast and conference platforms throughout the United States empowering women through her story and sharing of her expert knowledge as a business professional. For contribution to the arts and as a women owned business Ms. Abney is an awardee of the 2019 Shero Awards and is a 2019 Finalist Indie Author.

Ms. Abney is also the founder of Victory Leadership Group, Inc a nonprofit organization providing Leadership and Character Development services for those transitioning into the workforce. She has worked with local businesses, schools, city and state officials by providing workshops to empower communities socially, economically and financially. She continues to be active in the community as the VP of Business Affairs with the Greater Augusta Black Chamber of Commerce headquartered in Augusta, Ga to help small business owners gain access to revenue generating opportunities to grow their business.

An example of PERSEVERANCE and STICKTUITY for her family Ms. Abney hails from New York and currently resides in Hephzibah, Ga. She is the mother of two adult boys and one college daughter and a proud grandmother to one - which is her "why".

Learn more at www.liaabney.biz or email info@liaabneyllc.com.

Or follow Ms. Abney on Facebook, Twitter, LinkedIn and Instagram@liaabneyllc.

Ira Warren

Ira Warren is an ordain minister, actress, poet, singer, author and is the CEO of Molestation Epidemic. The native Texan now resided in Philadelphia, Pa with her husband John Warren and 3 of 10 children. Her husband and children are right behind her supporting her dreams. Her passion is to server and to bring awareness of child molestation to her community. One of the main things she lives by and love to express to people is her motto which is "overcome to become". Ira's vision is to make her organization Molestation Epidemic worldwide until every victim voice is heard.

Sherone Weeks

Sherone Weeks is a native of Maryland's Eastern Shore, who is passionate about advocacy for diverse and unique populations and considers herself a lifelong learner. She has four wonderful children, whom she affectionately refers to as "Thompson Enterprises". Being raised in a dedicated Christian home, by a no-nonsense single Mother, gave her the foundation to maintain drive, tenacity and to acknowledge God in ALL of her ways.

Sherone is currently a Behavioral Health Coordinator for the mental health authority agency, that covers the five mid-shore county region. She has a BS in Psychology from Towson University and is currently working toward a Master of

Human and Social Services with Walden University. Sherone can often be found in the community, involved in such efforts as voter registration, Board of Education meetings or bringing attention to disparities and disproportionalities of services for people of color. Sherone lives by the Scripture verse that declares "with God, ALL things are possible"! She is a firm Believer that empowering individuals and families with resources and education, is the key to improving our communities.

Robin M. Sample

Robin M. Sample is a best-selling author, motivational speaker and advocate or victims of domestic violence, sexual assault and trauma. She is a native of Cambridge, MD, born to Cynthia L. and the late Robert M. Sampson. She is the mother of two beautiful children, Ronald Jr. (Aiesha) and JaQuaya Beasley and the grandmother of five amazing jewels, Za'Meira, Zion, NaShon, Dominique (Doodle Bug) and Camden (Turtle). Robin's first book, "When I Stopped Being Angry with God", was released in June 2016 and her writing career has soared since that time. Her second book, "21 Affirmations for Forgiveness and Healing", was released in March 2017. Her third book, "The Breaking to Brilliance", is a collaboration project, written under the leadership of Dr. Valeka Moore, and her fourth book, Little Girls' Dreams Metamorphosis to Women's Realities", also a collaboration project, written under the leadership of Author Michelle Boulden Hammond, were both released in2019. Robin is currently in the process of writing her fifth book, which is the follow-up to her first book and she is also a part of a collaboration project, "Polished, Passionate and Poised", both due to be released later in 2019. Robin's story of having survived domestic violence will be featured in the "She Wins" Documentary, which is also due to be released later in 2019. Robin is a contributing writer for Heels Global Magazine and was recently featured in the 'Authors on The Move' segment in "All About Inspire" magazine. Robin is a 1988 graduate of Cambridge-South Dorchester High School, a 2002 graduate of Chesapeake College, having earned an A.A.S. Degree in Paralegal Studies, and a 2005 graduate of Washington College, having earned a B.A. Degree in Psychology. She recently graduated Magna Cum Laude from Widener University, on May 17, 2019, having earned a Master's Degree in Social Work. Robin also completed the Advanced Trauma Treatment Level I training from The Institute for Advanced Psychotherapy Training and Education, Inc. in June 2016. Robin is currently employed as the Case Management Coordinator for Mid-Shore Council on Family Violence, where she spends her days providing advocacy, support and counseling services to victims of Domestic Violence. She is also an independent sales consultant for Paparazzi Jewelry. Robin's prior employment experiences include time spent as a Victim Advocate & Community Outreach Coordinator with For All Seasons, Inc./Rape Crisis Center, Addictions Counselor with the Caroline Counseling Center and Family

Advocate with the Dorchester Early Learning Center. Robin is a commissioner on the Board of Zoning Appeals for Dorchester County and she is a Co- Leader for Brownie Girl Troop #s 412, 523 and 138. Auth

Robin is very actively involved in her church, Union Chapel A.M.E. Church, where her pastor is Rev. Dana Porter-Ashton. Because of her relationship with God, Robin believes that her past was orchestrated to serve as a source of motivation and inspiration for others to also seek God in the midst of storms and trials. She also believes that her past and present work experiences collaboratively tell the story of who she was and who she was called to be. Robin is a woman with more than just a story to tell, she is a woman with a testimony, a dream and a passion, a passion to inspire others to never give up. She is a living testimony of how low self-esteem, poor body image, lack of self-confidence, lack of self-worth, promiscuity, rejection, abandonment, bullying, alcohol dependence, multiple suicide attempts, domestic violence and sexual assault can be the very tests that give way to an amazing testimony of strength, courage, perseverance, hope and faith. "When I Stopped Being Angry With God" and Robin's other works will take you on a journey of how Robin's hurt, pain, brokenness and trauma, having left her feeling angry and resentful towards God for 31 years, has birthed a deep passion within her to inspire and motivate others to seek God in the midst of a storm.

Linette Howard

Linette Michelle Howard is a wife and a mother figure to my nephew and a freelance Christian makeup artist, and although she is challenged daily on trying to find ways to maneuver it all, and still succeed mentally, and physically and also accomplish the plans that God has created for her at the ripe young age of fifty, in lieu of her my newly created ministry. She says that she must admit that, although it does become a little overwhelming at times, but her philosophy is "If it doesn't challenge you, then it won't change you" and No pain, No gain". Having been born and raised in what used to be called "The Chocolate City" and also back in the 1990's was named the "Murder Capital", Washington D.C. has truly shaped and made Linette into the strong, black and beautiful woman that she is today. She was raised in a single parent home by her mother, along with her other three siblings, she had no father figure to go to for anything, and so she had to figure things out on her own. While she did get quite a few bumps and permanent bruises along the way, she says with an immense amount of joy and gratefulne ss, that she wouldn't change a thing and that all of those bumps and bruises have made her the woman that she is today. Polished, Passionate & Poised Linette Michelle Howard is ready to share with the world how at Fifty, she is now Poised by Grace.

Dr. Tasheka Green

Dr. Tasheka L. Green is a transformational servant leader who leads with the heart of a servant but the mind of a leader. She views leadership not as a job or career, but a calling with a greater purpose. Dr. Green has over 18-years of experience as an educator. She is an inspirational speaker, influential coach, eight-time author, entrepreneur, philanthropist, talk show host, and the Founder, President, and Chief Executive Officer of To Everything There is a Season, Incorporated which comprises of the following entities: The Deborah C. Offer Bulgin Business and Leadership Development Institute, To Everything There Is a Season Publishing, The Deborah C.

Offer Bulgin Memorial Foundation, Women of Virtue Walking in Excellence Awards, Signature by William Green, and I am a QT...Queen in Training.

She serves with a focus to support individuals and organizations in identifying the gifts and talents within themselves and providing them with the systems, structures, and resources to fulfill their purpose.

Her innovative coaching techniques influences personal, professional development, and organizational change. Because of her competency with bringing coherence to improving culture, systems, structures, and people, Dr. Green is sought after by many. The work of Dr. Green garnered her a feature in the Harvard University School of Education, HarvardX Course, Introduction to Data Wise: A Collaborative Process to Improve Learning & Teaching.

A scholarly and virtuous woman of extraordinary faith, vision, talents, presence, and accomplishments, have allowed her to obtain a plethora of recognitions and awards. Dr. Green is an example of when preparation meets opportunity, the end result is success. She loves God and radiates with the joy of the Lord.

Dr. Green is married to William Z. Green Sr, and they have three beautiful children, Marquis, Mikayla, and William Jr.

Lynda D. Mallory

Hi, my name is **Lynda D. Mallory** and I am an accidental writer. Why? Well, because writing helped me get through a tough time a few years ago and now I love to write and inspire people to be great, no matter what their current situation looks like. I help people adopt a positive lifestyle and outlook because this mindset has made all the difference for me through my own ups and downs.I began writing when I was nine years old. I came up with characters based on what I wanted to be when I grew up; this even included being a super hero! I have always had a creative side and I wanted to bridge my creativeness and find ways to help others through life's challenges. This is where the concept of A Life With A View was born in July 2013. As a blogger and author, I have been thrilled to meet like-minded bloggers, writers and creative coaches along the way, who share my passion for inspiring others. "Be honest about who you are and remain true to yourself. Embrace your whole self; your emotions, your faith, your vulnerabilities. Don't be afraid of the journey. It will define and motivate you to be your best." — Lynda D. Mallory If you have ever struggled with self-confidence, knowing your self-worth, establishing your faith and renewal, you are in the right place. Join me on this journey while I provide you resources to help you get through the good and not so good times. For a more consolidated view of inspiration, stop by and take a peek and purchase my first book: A Life With A View. This book has my most precious blog posts when I began blogging.

Speaking of blog posts, be sure to subscribe here on my webpage and connect with me on social media. Here on my webpage, you will find information about the book publishing process, blog posts for tips on sharing your writings, and also a resource library to help you through every aspect of your writing and business. I look forward to bringing you inspirational resources to help and guide you find your life with a view.

Made in the USA
Lexington, KY
29 November 2019